50+ Icons Your Grandparents Would Not Have Understood When They Were Young

A look at the icons that define our everyday technological lives and when they became popular.

Note for Tablets
All icons are in black and transparent. If your background on your tablet is black with white letters, you will not be able to see the icons.

This collection will not include what we may consider to be familiar icons but that are business logos. Examples of such icons include but are not limited to:

However, some companies will be mentioned for their innovative product that made these icons possible.
Also ignored will be other pop culture icons as they are derived from artistic works and not symbolic of items we interact with on a daily basis. Examples of such icons include but are not limited to:

Scientific icons, such as units of measurements will be ignored, as well as cultural behaviors, such as hand-shakes.

Finally, all religious, mythological and political symbols will also be ignored. Examples of such icons include but are not limited to:

Note about the selection of these icons:
While a lot of these iconic devices or 'things' may have been invented much further back in history, such as the headphones, they were not widely used by the general public until approximately the dates

presented in this book. Some of these may have been invented further back than what was also originally expected.

Table of Contents

Prologue

The overall goal of this publication is to demonstrate how in such a short span of time our way of life has evolved; if we were to pluck your grand-parent from their early life to bring them to ours, these symbols that we take for granted would either not be understood or mean very different things.

While we have become accustomed to this in our ever-evolving world, it's important to remember that for the large majority of human history, a lot of the technologies used remained relatively the same over many generations. The parents of our grandparents lived in a similar fashion to their parents. Our grandparents are the last to have grown up in a world where it was understood that their descendants would live a similar life as they had, technologically.

Our parents are the first generation that have grown up with technological tools that have changed every few years, becoming smaller, more interactive, allowing them to live more private lives (the Walkman, for example, allowed people to listen to the music they wanted to, not the music the rest of the people in the room wanted to).

What symbols will our children invent to represent the next leap in technologies? Because we are here for the evolution, we will most likely understand the icons, but if we were to be teleported to the future, would we be able to make sense of these ideograms? Or would we be like the archeologists that re-discovered ancient Egyptian hieroglyphs?

The goal is to reflect on how these icons seem ubiquitous today but to a teenager from the early 20th century, these would mean nothing (or at least something very different).

All these icons (with the exception of the passport) were developed in the middle of the 20th century or later.

Fun method:

The title of the icon is not presented until halfway down the page. If you want to guess and test your skills, cover the bottom half of your page as you flip through the book.

1920

Passport control was codified by the Paris Conference on Passports & Customs Formalities and Through Tickets, a conference organized by the League of Nations in 1920 which agreed, for the first time, on a set of standards for all passports issued by members of the League. Prior to that time, there were no internationally agreed standards for passports because they were not generally required for travel until World War I.[1]

1946

The international radiation symbol (also known as the trefoil) first appeared in 1946. The sign is commonly referred to as a radioactivity warning sign, and became well known during the Cold War due to the threat of nuclear war.[2] The most common sign for danger prior to this symbol to signal danger was the skull and crossbones, still in use today.

1952

The term double helix refers to the structure formed by double-stranded molecules of nucleic acids such as DNA. The double helix model of DNA was discovered in 1952.[3]

1964

■ ❚❚ ▶

◀◀ ▶▶

◀❚ ▲ ❚▶

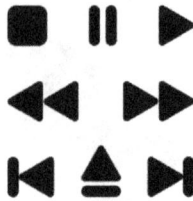

In digital electronics, analogue electronics and entertainment, the user interface of media may include media controls or player controls, to enact and change or adjust the process of watching film or listening to audio.[4]

1966

A heated seat is a seat that is heated to certain temperatures inside a car. The first production car with the option for heated seats was the 1966 Cadillac DeVille.[5]

1967

Payment cards are part of a payment system issued by financial institutions, such as a bank, to a customer that enables its owner (the cardholder) to access the funds in the customer's designated bank accounts, or through a credit account and make payments by electronic funds transfer and access automated teller machines (ATMs). The first bank cards were ATM cards issued by Barclays in London in 1967.[6]

1967

An automated teller machine (ATM) is an electronic telecommunications device that enables customers of financial institutions to perform financial transactions, such as cash withdrawals, deposits, transfer funds, or obtaining account information, at any time and without the need for direct interaction with bank staff. It is widely accepted that the first cash machine was put into use by Barclays Bank in its Enfield Town branch in North London, United Kingdom, on 27 June 1967.[7]

1970

Recycling has been a process conducted since the dawn of time, however, the universal recycling logo was created in 1970. Container Corporation of America, a large producer of recycled paperboard, sponsored a contest for art and design students at high schools and colleges across the United States to raise awareness of environmental issues. It was won by Gary Anderson, then a 23-year-old college student at the University of Southern California, whose entry was the image now known as the universal recycling symbol.[8]

1970

Commercial air travel was not a novelty in 1970, having existed for some time prior, but wide, affordable access to the general population did not occur until the introduction of the Boeing 747 in 1970. This accelerated the social changes brought about by the Jet Age and introduced these icons to the population.[9]

1971

An electronic calculator is typically a portable electronic device used to perform calculations, ranging from basic arithmetic to complex mathematics. However, integrated circuit development efforts culminated in early 1971 with the introduction of the first "calculator on a chip", the MK6010 by Mostek, followed by Texas Instruments later in the year. Although these early hand-held calculators were very costly, these advances in electronics, together with developments in display technology led within a few years to the cheap pocket calculator available to all.[10]

1972

Seatbelts aboard commercial aircraft were mandated by the US Federal Aviation Administration in 1972.[11]

1973

The power symbol is a symbol indicating that a control activates or deactivates a particular device. Although electronic devices for individual use had already been available for about 25 years, the power symbol as universally accepted today was described for the first time in the International Electrotechnical Commission 60417 standard in 1973.[12]

1979

While headphones were invented early in the 20th century, they were only used by the US navy, telephone and radio operators, and individuals in similar industries. The 3.5 mm radio and phone connector, saw the headphone popularity reinforced with its use on the massively popular Walkman portable tape player in 1979.[13]

1981

A barcode (also bar code) is an optical, machine-readable representation of data; the data usually describes something about the object that carries the barcode. Invented in 1949, it wasn't until the late 1970s that IBM worked the barcode for use as the Universal Product Code. In 1981, the United States Department of Defense adopted the use of the barcode and Code 39 for marking all products sold to the United States military. This system is widely viewed as the catalyst for widespread adoption of barcoding.[14]

1982

A personal computer (PC) is a multi-purpose computer whose size, capabilities, and price make it feasible for individual use. Personal computers are intended to be operated directly by an end user, rather than by a computer expert or technician. While around for a number of years, it wasn't until 1982 that computers reached mass appeal instead of being restricted to highly specialized fields. That same year, "The Computer" was named Machine of the Year by Time magazine.[15]

1983

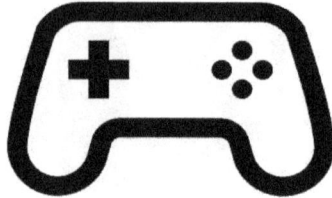

A video game console is a computer device that outputs a video signal or visual image to display a video game that one or more people can play. While the first generation of video game consoles appeared in the late 1960s, it wasn't after the North American video game crash of 1983 with the release of third generation consoles and the release of the Nintendo NES in 1983 that video game consoles gained wide consumer appeal.[16]

1983

Radio-frequency identification (RFID) uses electromagnetic fields to automatically identify and track tags attached to objects. First patented in 1983, the miniaturization of RFID chips at the start of the 21st century have made them ever present for a variety of uses, from tracking supplies, toll-systems, and even injected into the human body to unlock various systems.

1984

The printer as a peripheral device makes a persistent human-readable representation of graphics or text on paper. The introduction of the low-cost laser printer in 1984 with the first HP LaserJet set off a revolution in printing known as desktop publishing.[17]

1984

A computer mouse is a hand-held pointing device that detects two-dimensional motion relative to a surface. This motion is typically translated into the motion of a pointer on a display, which allows a smooth control of the graphical user interface. The first public demonstration of a mouse controlling a computer system was in 1968. The mouse remained relatively obscure until the appearance of the Macintosh 128K (which included an updated version of the Lisa Mouse) in 1984.[18]

1987

911 is an emergency telephone number for the North American Numbering Plan (NANP). While the first 911 call was made in 1958, it wasn't until 1987 that 50% of Americans could dial the number for emergency services. By 2000, it was 93%.[19]

1989

A keyless entry system is an electronic lock that controls access to a building or vehicle without using a traditional mechanical key. One of the first introductions was in 1980 on specific Ford vehicles. The feature gained its first widespread availability in the U.S. on several General Motors vehicles in 1989. In the early 2000s, electronic keys gained popularity to start cars and access personal homes.[20]

1989

A handheld game console, or simply handheld console, is a small, portable self-contained video game console with a built-in screen, game controls, and speakers. Nintendo is credited with popularizing the handheld console concept with the release of the Game Boy in 1989, even though version of handheld game consoles existed as early as 1979.[21]

1989

A rechargeable battery, storage battery, secondary cell, or accumulator is a type of electrical battery which can be charged, discharged into a load, and recharged many times, as opposed to a disposable or primary battery, which is supplied fully charged and discarded after use. Re-chargeable battery development in the 1980s allowed the future development of mobile phones and other small devices. Re-chargeable nickel-metal hydride were common for consumers by 1989 and subsequently into the 1990s. The advent of lithium-ion batteries became apparent to consumers in the early 2000s as gadgets became smaller and more powerful.[22]

1991

A laptop is a small, portable personal computer with a "clamshell" form factor, having, typically, a thin computer screen mounted on the inside of the upper lid and an alphanumeric keyboard on the inside of the lower lid. The world's "first mass-market laptop computer" was the Toshiba T1100, released in 1985. However, laptops in their most similar form to today did not become mainstream until 1991, when color screens became standard on the devices.

1991

Antivirus software, or anti-virus software (abbreviated to AV software), also known as anti-malware, is a computer program used to prevent, detect, and remove malware. Although the roots of the computer virus date back as early as 1949, when the Hungarian scientist John von Neumann published the "Theory of self-reproducing automata", it wasn't until 1991 that the first commercial anti-virus software was released in the United States.[23]

1991

The at sign, a part of every SMTP email address. Electronic mail (email) is a method of exchanging messages ("mail") between people using electronic devices.[24] The @ sign has existed since at least 1345, but has not been widely used until the advent of the e-mail in the early 1990s, with Microsoft Mail's release in 1991 becoming the new standard.

1993

and

In computing, a hyperlink, or simply a link, is a reference to data that the reader can directly follow either by clicking or tapping. In 1990, Windows Help, which was introduced with Microsoft Windows 3.0, had widespread use of hyperlinks to link different pages in a single help file together. The first widely used open protocol that included hyperlinks was the 1991 Gopher protocol. It was soon eclipsed by HTML after the 1993 release of the Mosaic browser, which had the ability to mix graphics, text, and hyperlinks.[25]

1993

A satellite is an artificial object which has been intentionally placed into orbit. While the first satellite was launched in 1957, to most of the world's interaction with a satellite began with satellite communications (including television). In 1994, 3 US companies all began satellite services when spacecraft technologies reach a viable cost, starting the commercial competition that would make satellite TV available to the world and boosting worldwide use of satellite use, along with GPS soon after.[26]

1994

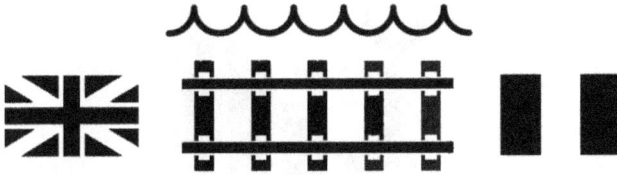

The Channel Tunnel is a 50.45-kilometre (31.35 mi) rail tunnel linking the United Kingdom with France, beneath the English Channel sea, allowing ground transportation between an the British Isles and continental Europe.[27]

1994

A mobile phone signal is the signal strength (measured in dBm) received by a mobile phone from a cellular network.[28] While 1983 saw the introduction of the Motorola DynaTAC, widely considered the first mobile phone, it wasn't until the 1994 Motorola International 8700 and 1996 Motorola StarTAC that screens on mobile phones displaying service signal gained widespread consumer adoption.[29]

1995

The Navstar Global Positioning System (GPS) is a satellite-based radio navigation system operated by the United States Air Force. It is a global navigation satellite system that provides geolocation and time information to a GPS receiver anywhere on or near the Earth where there is an unobstructed line of sight to four or more GPS satellites.[30] First seeing widespread commercial application in cars and portable navigation systems in the mid-1990s, modern life now relies on GPS, with stock-markets, smartphones and the Internet infrastructure on the GPS signal.

1995

The Internet (contraction of interconnected network) is the global system of interconnected computer networks that use the Internet protocol suite (TCP/IP) to link devices worldwide. Since 1995 the Internet has tremendously impacted culture and commerce, including the rise of near instant communication by email, instant messaging, and the World Wide Web with its discussion forums, blogs, social networking, and online shopping sites.[31]

1995

The universally accepted icons to control various application presentations on computers first appeared on the Microsoft Windows 95 interface.

1995

Download means to receive data from a remote system, typically a server such as a web server, an FTP server, an email server, or other similar systems.[32]

1995

Solar power is the conversion of energy from sunlight into electricity, either directly using photovoltaics (PV), indirectly using concentrated solar power, or a combination. Invented 1860, the 1% efficiency of the solar cells at the time made them impractical for general use. In the mid-1990s, development of both, residential and commercial rooftop solar as well as utility-scale photovoltaic power stations, began to accelerate again due to supply issues with oil and natural gas, global warming concerns, and the improving economic position of PV relative to other energy technologies.[33]

1996

```
:-)  :-(   :-/    :-O  :'-(   :-D
:)   :(    :*)     :O  :-{}  :'(  8-)
!-) :-x  ;-)   @}->--    ;)   :-#
```

An emoticon short for "emotion icon", is a pictorial representation of a facial expression using characters – usually punctuation marks, numbers, and letters – to express a person's feelings or mood, or as a time-saving method. The first ASCII emoticons, :-) and :-(were written by Scott Fahlman in 1982. As SMS and the internet became widespread in the late 1990s, emoticons became increasingly popular and were commonly used on text messages, internet forums and e-mails. Emoticons offer another range of "tone" and feeling through texting that portrays specific emotions through facial gestures while in the midst of text-based cyber communication. Emoticons evolved into modern day emojis.[34]

1997

MP3 is a digital coding format for digital audio that reduces (or approximates) the accuracy of certain components of sound that are considered to be beyond the hearing capabilities of most humans, allowing files to be 91% smaller than a CD file. Invented in 1993, the MP3 became popular with the advent of the Internet and sharing sites like Napster and KaZaA where users shared music over slow-speed connections.[35]

1998

Bluetooth is a wireless technology standard for exchanging data over short distances using short-wavelength UHF radio waves in the ISM band from 2.400 to 2.485 GHz from fixed and mobile devices. While invented in 1994, specifications for Bluetooth weren't detailed until 1998.[36]

1998

USB (abbreviation of Universal Serial Bus) is an industry standard that establishes specifications for cables, connectors and protocols for connection, communication and power supply between personal computers and their peripheral devices. It was invented in 1996 but few USB devices made it to the market until USB 1.1 was released in August 1998.[37]

1999

Wi-Fi is technology for radio wireless local area networking of devices based on the IEEE 802.11 standards.[38]

1999

SMS (short message service) is a text messaging service component of most telephone, internet, and mobile-device systems. The protocols allowed users to send and receive messages of up to 160 alpha-numeric characters to and from GSM mobiles. The first SMS message was sent in 1992, and while initial growth was slow in 1995, by 1999, usage had exploded when carriers allowed SMS exchanges with other carriers. With the evolution of technology, by 2018 people no longer referred to these short messages as SMS, but as texts.[39]

2000

Active noise cancelling headphones were first developed in a useful prototype in 1986 before being commercially available in 1989. Bose's commercialization of active noise cancelling headphones helped propel the technology into ubiquity 2000.[40]

2002

The Euro is the official currency of 19 member states of the European Union as of 2018. The euro is the second largest and second most traded currency in the foreign exchange market after the United States dollar. It came into circulation 1 January 2002, replacing the original currency of the member states including but not limited to the following the following currencies[41]:

Franc
Finish markka
German Mark
Irish pound
Italian and Vatican Lira
Spanish Peseta

2003

Videotelephony comprises the technologies for the reception and transmission of audio-video signals by users at different locations, for communication between people in real-time. Invented in the 1920s and refined by NASA for use in manned spaceflight, it wasn't until the 2000s, videotelephony was popularized via free Internet services such as Skype and iChat, web plugins and on-line telecommunication programs that promoted low cost videoconferencing to virtually every location with an Internet connection.[42]

2006

Cloud storage is a model of computer data storage in which the digital data is stored in multiple servers (sometimes in multiple locations), and the physical environment is typically owned and managed by a hosting company, while the user uploads and downloads data onto the server through a network. In 1994, AT&T launched PersonaLink Services, an online platform for personal and business communication and entrepreneurship. The storage was one of the first to be all web-based, but it wasn't until Amazon.com developed its web services in 2006 that cloud companies started to thrive.[43]

2007

A voice-user interface (VUI) makes spoken human interaction with computers possible, using speech recognition to understand spoken commands and questions, and typically text to speech to play a reply. Windows Vista was the first mass market software to include voice command, and in 2010, Android 2.2 "Froyo" was the first operating system for mobile devices to include a VUI.[44]

2007

A touchscreen, or touch screen, is an input device and normally layered on the top of an electronic visual display of an information processing system. While touchscreens gained popularity in the late 1990s with the stylus controlled personal digital assistants, the aggressive advent of smartphones (like the LG Prada) in 2007.[45]

2008

An e-reader, also called an e-book reader or e-book device, is a mobile electronic device that is designed primarily for the purpose of reading digital e-books and periodicals. Different than a normal computer tablet that is simply a smartphone with a bigger screen, e-readers use an e-ink display that replicate the appearance of ordinary ink on paper. E-ink was created in 1997 and the first e-reader was released in 2004 by Sony. However, the Amazon Kindle started the revolutionary use of e-readers when it was released in 2007 and became popular in 2008 thanks to their innovative book-sales infrastructure.[46]

2008

An electric car is a plug-in electric automobile that is propelled by one or more electric motors, using energy typically stored in rechargeable batteries. While the first production electric vehicle was rolled out 1884, internal combustion engines soon dominated the marked. However, since 2008, a renaissance in electric vehicle manufacturing occurred due to advances in batteries, concerns about increasing oil prices, and the desire to reduce greenhouse gas emissions.[47]

2009

A cryptocurrency (or crypto currency) is a digital asset designed to work as a medium of exchange that uses strong cryptography to secure financial transactions, control the creation of additional units, and verify the transfer of assets. Bitcoin, first released as open-source software in 2009, is generally considered the first decentralized cryptocurrency.[48]

2010

Near-field communication (NFC) is a set of communication protocols that enable two electronic devices, one of which is usually a portable device such as a smartphone, to establish communication by bringing them within 4 cm (1.6 in) of each other.[49]

2014

An unmanned aerial vehicle (UAV), commonly known as a drone, is an aircraft without a human pilot aboard. While the military has used much more sophisticated systems for over a decade, drones really took off in the commercial world in 2014 when many companies started to use them to conduct aerial photography and films.[50]

2015

360-degree videos or pictures, also known as immersive videos or picture, are image recordings where a view in every direction is recorded at the same time, shot using an omnidirectional camera or a collection of cameras. During playback on normal flat display the viewer has control of the viewing direction like a panorama. The format gained popularity in 2015 when the popular video-sharing site YouTube began support for this format.[51]

2016

Virtual reality (VR) is an interactive computer-generated experience taking place within a simulated environment. While the first common device, the Oculus Rift, was release in 2010, in 2016, HTC shipped its first units of the HTC Vive SteamVR headset. This marked the first major commercial release of sensor-based tracking, allowing for free movement of users within a defined space. Regardless, haptic interfaces were not well developed by the mid-2010s, and most hardware packages incorporated button-operated handsets for touch-based interactivity. Visually, displays were still of a low-enough resolution and frame rate that images were still identifiable as virtual.[52]

2017

A self-driving car, also known as a robot car, autonomous car, or driverless car, is a vehicle that is capable of sensing its environment and moving with little or no human input. Technologies such as adaptive cruise control and more have been developed in the early 2000s, however in 2017, Waymo was the first company to utilize driverless cars without a safety driver in the driver position.[53]

Obsolescent Icons

These are icons that are still utilized today but that may have their original meaning become outdated (or it already is) or they may be icons that today have new meaning:

Floppy Disk

A floppy disk is a type of disk storage composed of a disk of thin and flexible magnetic storage medium, sealed in a rectangular plastic enclosure lined with fabric that removes dust particles. Invented in 1975, floppy disks became commonplace during the 1980s and 1990s in their use with personal computers to distribute software, transfer data, and create backups. By 2006, floppy disks were rarely manufactured anymore, but the prevalence of floppy disks in late-twentieth century culture was such that many electronic and software programs still use the floppy disks as save icons.[54]

Film

A film, also called a movie or motion picture is a series of still images that, when shown on a screen, create the illusion of moving images. While existing in some fashion for thousands of years, it's the Golden Age of Hollywood from the 1920s to the 1960s brought upon the film icon that lasts even today. However, most films today are recorded using digital means, even if the icon endures.[55]

Fax

Fax (short for facsimile) is the telephonic transmission of scanned printed material (both text and images. Becoming popular in the late 1970s, fax machines today, while still prevalent, are being more and more replaced by Internet-based technologies around the modern word (with one exception being Japan, which continues to use faxes extensively).[56]

Cassettes

+

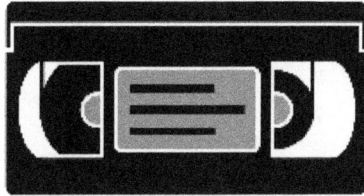

The cassette tape is an analog magnetic tape-recording format for audio recording and playback. It was developed and released in 1962. During the 1990s, CDs overtook cassettes as the preferred playback medium.[57] VHS (short for Video Home System) is a standard for consumer-level analog video recording on tape cassettes. Although developed in 1977, it only became the universal cassette player format after the Betamax vs. VHS format war ended in the early 1980s. By the early 2000s, the format was replaced by DVDs and later on by Blu-ray.[58]

Search Engine

A search engine is a software system that is designed to carry out a search on the Internet. By 2000, the majority of the market was delineated between three major companies: Google, Yahoo! and Microsoft. The search engine icon today is most commonly a magnifying glass.[59]

Mobile Phone

This is an icon that became prevalent in the mid-1990s, but by the mid-2000s came to represent a device that has similar functions but does not look the same (see the more modern icon below to represent a *smart*phone).

Iconic Expressions

While these are not pictorial, they are terms and expressions that today demonstrate how in 100 years or less, a lot of our vocabulary has evolved to reference items that didn't exist not long ago.

Not included in these will be cultural expression that reflect mindsets created by the current geopolitical realities (such as "Made in China") as these change all the time. Nor will these be references to individuals (such as "Thanks, Einstein!") as these may be generational, as well. Finally, these will not include current pop culture references (such as "mad cool" or "that's OP") because these are cultural niche expressions.

This list is not all inclusive and is only meant to represent how fast technological evolutions have changed the way we communicate compared to only a few generations ago.

I'll text you.

Email me.

S/he swipped right.

Where's the remote?

I don't have service.

My number is…

Stream it today!

This isn't the Moon race.

Log on today!

Drop it on your desktop.

There's an app for that.

My flight's at…

References

[1] https://en.wikipedia.org/wiki/Passport
[2] https://en.wikipedia.org/wiki/Hazard_symbol#Radioactive_sign
[3] https://en.wikipedia.org/wiki/Nucleic_acid_double_helix
[4] https://en.wikipedia.org/wiki/Media_controls
[5] https://www.caranddriver.com/features/g15382751/automotive-firsts-the-first-production-cars-with-turbocharging-navigation-heated-seats-and-more/?slide=14
[6] https://en.wikipedia.org/wiki/Payment_card
[7] https://en.wikipedia.org/wiki/Automated_teller_machine
[8] https://en.wikipedia.org/wiki/Recycling_symbol
[9] https://en.wikipedia.org/wiki/Jet_Age
[10] https://en.wikipedia.org/wiki/Calculator
[11] https://www.atlasobscura.com/articles/why-are-airplane-seatbelts-so-weird
[12] https://en.wikipedia.org/wiki/Power_symbol
[13] https://en.wikipedia.org/wiki/Headphones
[14] https://en.wikipedia.org/wiki/Barcode
[15] https://en.wikipedia.org/wiki/Personal_computer
[16] https://en.wikipedia.org/wiki/Video_game_console
[17] https://en.wikipedia.org/wiki/Printer_(computing)
[18] https://en.wikipedia.org/wiki/Computer_mouse
[19] https://en.wikipedia.org/wiki/9-1-1
[20] https://en.wikipedia.org/wiki/Remote_keyless_system
[21] https://en.wikipedia.org/wiki/Handheld_game_console
[22] https://en.wikipedia.org/wiki/Rechargeable_battery
[23] https://en.wikipedia.org/wiki/Antivirus_software
[24] https://en.wikipedia.org/wiki/Email
[25] https://en.wikipedia.org/wiki/Hyperlink
[26] https://en.wikipedia.org/wiki/Satellite_television
[27] https://en.wikipedia.org/wiki/Channel_Tunnel
[28] https://en.wikipedia.org/wiki/Mobile_phone_signal
[29] https://en.wikipedia.org/wiki/Motorola_StarTAC
[30] https://en.wikipedia.org/wiki/Global_Positioning_System
[31] https://en.wikipedia.org/wiki/Internet
[32] https://en.wikipedia.org/wiki/Download
[33] https://en.wikipedia.org/wiki/Solar_power
[34] https://en.wikipedia.org/wiki/Emoticon
[35] https://en.wikipedia.org/wiki/MP3
[36] https://en.wikipedia.org/wiki/Bluetooth
[37] https://en.wikipedia.org/wiki/USB
[38] https://en.wikipedia.org/wiki/Wi-Fi
[39] https://en.wikipedia.org/wiki/SMS
[40] https://en.wikipedia.org/wiki/Active_noise_control
[41] https://en.wikipedia.org/wiki/Euro
[42] https://en.wikipedia.org/wiki/Videotelephony
[43] https://en.wikipedia.org/wiki/Cloud_storage
[44] https://en.wikipedia.org/wiki/Voice_user_interface
[45] https://en.wikipedia.org/wiki/Touchscreen
[46] https://en.wikipedia.org/wiki/E-reader
[47] https://en.wikipedia.org/wiki/Electric_car
[48] https://en.wikipedia.org/wiki/Cryptocurrency
[49] https://en.wikipedia.org/wiki/Near-field_communication

[50] https://en.wikipedia.org/wiki/Unmanned_aerial_vehicle
[51] https://en.wikipedia.org/wiki/360-degree_video
[52] https://en.wikipedia.org/wiki/Virtual_reality
[53] https://en.wikipedia.org/wiki/Self-driving_car
[54] https://en.wikipedia.org/wiki/Floppy_disk
[55] https://en.wikipedia.org/wiki/Film
[56] https://en.wikipedia.org/wiki/Fax
[57] https://en.wikipedia.org/wiki/Cassette_tape
[58] https://en.wikipedia.org/wiki/VHS

[59] https://en.wikipedia.org/wiki/Web_search_engine